The Oranges of Sicily

A CULINARY HISTORY OF THE WORLD'S MOST IMPORTANT FRUIT

+ 30 CURIOUS RECIPES

Texts by Vinci Bellomo
Photos by Antonino Bartuccio e Alessandro Saffo

SIMEBOOKS

Amid the heady scent of brine that enhances the Gulf of Palermo, we find ourselves talking about citrus fruits, and, in particular, the orange: the true gold of Sicily that has flowed through the veins of Sicilians and the veins of the island's soil for centuries.

It is here that the orange was born as we know it, as we taste it and celebrate it today.

In Sicily, the orange, the lemon, and the mandarin find the microclimate to expand all of their qualities and richness. Specific properties prove especially helpful to health, such as the presence of ascorbic acid, better known as Vitamin C, a substance that combats the common cold and related illnesses. An orange weighing 150-200 grams (5-7 oz) supplies more than 100 percent of the daily recommended dose of Vitamin B1, essential for cardiac, muscular and nervous functioning, and the folic acid essential for tissue growth. Oranges also contain potassium, calcium, and a large amount of beta-cryptoxanthin, a powerful antioxidant, and lycopene with its strong antitumoral effect.

Many medicines are made from this marvelous tree. Already in the 16th century the bark of the orange, as well as the flower, fruit and leaves were used to prepare pharmaceutical products. The long list of prescriptions comes down to our own times. In 17th-century Sicily, to combat the various epidemics spreading through the island, people were advised to always carry an orange with them. At Scicli in Sicily, to combat epileptic seizures, the Capuchin fathers prepared an effective compound from the bark of the orange tree. There was also a stimulating elixir made from oranges, alcohol, and wine, while almond milk included orange juice. The peel had many uses, one being as a hair-restorer. This was a firm belief handed down through the centuries. In the villages of the Sicilian hinterland the orange compound was used to help hair regrowth: a few drops of orange juice on the hair worked the miracle. But even today, it's worth remembering, there are many pharmaceutical products based on oranges or lemons: throat pastilles, laxatives, nutritional supplements, and dietetic rice biscuits; and today, just as in past centuries, the orange is life. But let's take a step back, to go deeper and look at the origins of the world's finest and most celebrated fruit.

Table of Contents

History p. 14
Varieties and Territory p. 24
Cosmetics and Perfumes p. 28
Curiosities and Information p. 35
The Economy p. 50
Culture, Myths, and Legends p. 58
Health and Gastronomy p. 60
The Taste of Orange p. 65
Dishes & Salads p. 67
Desserts & Cocktails p. 117

History

The origins of oranges and citrus fruits in general, or at any rate the fruits belonging to the Rutaceae family, are lost in time. In China in 450 BC, in the middle of the Zhou dynasty, word spread through the valleys of the Yellow River of a round orange fruit. It was aesthetically perfect, with its white and fragrant flowers, its shape, and then those juicy and mysterious golden globes, a hymn to perfection, happiness and prosperity. The Chinese people immediately grasped the value of citrus fruits and began cultivating them throughout the eastern regions. Their uses were highly varied. The petals were collected and used to perfume linens; the fruits were offered to the emperor; and we can only imagine how its juice was enjoyed–but we can certainly say that the orange's most evident qualities were those that became known first. From China the next step took place in India, where they immediately discovered, appreciated, and understood the trees bearing yellow fruit: the lemon.

As far as genetic origins are concerned, it is now clear from the most accredited sources that there were four ancestors of citrus fruits: the pomelo, mandarin, citron (citrus medica) and mountain citron (citrus hulimii). The whole range of citrus fruits grew out of these species. A series of crosses between the pomelo and the mandarin gave rise to the common orange; between the citron and other species to the lemon; and grapefruit is derived from the pomelo. Thanks to the activities of the far-sighted Chinese traders and their desire to understand and spread their knowledge, with the passing of the centuries citrus fruits spread to Europe, finding their perfect environment in Sicily.

As early as the twelfth century there are records of the production of sweet and bitter oranges in Sicily. Even further back in time there is evidence of the cultivation of the bitter orange under the Arab domination (827-1072). In 1094, a document of Roger the Norman already speaks of the existence of a *Via Arangeriis*, with streets and gardens with citrus trees that adorned and perfumed the Islamic houses, glowing spheres with bright colors that enriched villas and palaces–a culture the endured even in the centuries following the Arab domination. In this way Sicily became a cradle for the creation and development of a unique fruit and perhaps the one most highly prized worldwide, with a fleshy rind, rich, full color, sweet and juicy, and with wonderful nutritional qualities. The spread of citrus orchards gave rise to the Conca d'Oro around Palermo.

The orange, the lemon, and the mandarin, evoke the sun and identify Sicily as the land of citrus fruit, which, thanks to the fortune of a perfect climate and the passions of men and women, has far more than any other identified itself with these products. Even though they arrived from far away, they are now identified in our imaginations as 100 percent Sicilian products.

Among the most incisive words that best describe and trace a very precise idea of what Sicily was in the Conca d'Oro, we can quote Sigmund Freud. In September 1910 he arrived in Palermo and wrote ecstatically to his wife Martha: "Such a wealth of colors, such views, so many fragrant smells, and such a sensation of well-being" (from *Letters of Sigmund Freud*, edited by Ernst L. Jones, Dover Books, 1960). Another traveler worth quoting was Goethe, who arrived in Palermo in 1787 and was fascinated to the point of writing,

"No words can express the hazy brilliancy which hung around the coasts, as on a most beautiful noon we neared Palermo. The purity of the outlines, the sweetness of the whole, the delicately changing shades of color, the harmony of the sky, the sea, the land... He who has once seen it will never forget it."

And he continues:

"Our welcome is beyond description - with its fresh green mulberry trees, evergreen oleanders, and hedges of citrons, etc. In the open gardens you see large beds of ranunculi and anemones. The air is mild, warm, and fragrant; the wind refreshing. The full moon, too, rose from behind a promontory, and shone upon the sea."

The landscape that appeared to the German poet was of rare beauty, harmonious and aesthetically perfect. The plain of the Conca d'Oro, extending over a hundred square kilometers, with its intense scents and colors, was formed six million years ago by the exhalation and separation of the chemical elements of the Mediterranean: a long, slow morphological upheaval that, through earthquakes, volcanic eruptions, and sea rises led to the birth of magical places such as Mount Pellegrino, the Madonie, and the hills overlooking the city of Palermo. A fertile land of oranges, lemons, and tangerines, it fills the days with color. The rich red earth is proud to host noble roots and from here spreads throughout Europe. Citrus fruit was grown as a symbol of wealth and abundance in immense, open-air gardens irrigated with works and methods dating back to Muslim times. All this was abruptly ended in the 1970s, when speculative development began in Palermo and the citrus groves were turned into 30-story buildings. Today, after years of battles, the uncontrolled wildcat development has been blocked and the Conca d'Oro has finally been protected, saving 25 percent of its original extent. If you go to Palermo, you can still visit the citrus-growing area in the Parco della Favorita, 230 hectares redolent of lemons and mandarins. It is a small, happy island at the foot of Mount Pellegrino, an ancient landscape indifferent to the evolutionary progress of humanity, where biological diversity is a reality, thanks to the favorable ecological factors. Pablo Neruda depicted the orange and lemon in perfect verse:

ODE TO THE ORANGE
In your likeness,
in your image,
orange,
the world was made:
round the sun, surrounded
to split itself with fire:
the night dotted with orange flowers
its route and its ship ...

ODE TO THE LEMON
Out of lemon flowers
loosed on the moonlight,
love's lashed and insatiable
essences,
sodden with fragrance,
the lemon tree's yellow
emerges, the lemons move down
from the tree's planetarium ...

Varieties and Territory

Naranja in Portugal, orange in England, *turuncu* in Turkey, *apel'sin* in Russia, *apfelsine* in Denmark, *oransje* in Norway and then *aranzovy, pomarancovy, portocala* and *pomarancza*: when we speak about citrus fruits, the whole of Europe is tinged with orange. If we turn to the Accademia della Crusca, the correct name in Italian appears to be *melarancia* or *melarancio*, but in common parlance, both the form *arancio* (orange tree) and *arancia* (the fruit), are appropriate.

As we have said, citrus fruits are among the best-selling fruits worldwide. The orange, lemon, or mandarin, with their attractive forms, juiciness, and sweet pulp, as well as their undoubted other properties, have long been a worldwide success. As far as the old continent is concerned, the orange in particular is the best-selling citrus fruit. The Sicilian blood orange is one of the biggest-selling citrus fruits in Italy and is much sought-after throughout Europe. The story of the red Sicilian orange is worthy of note. This variant developed as a random mutation, a sport of nature that grew under the hot sun of Sicily, giving rise to a fruit that today alone accounts for 60 percent of the market. The colored molecules contained in the red orange are the cause of this reddish pigmentation, which, in addition to its obvious aesthetic pleasure, contains outstanding healthy properties.

Citruses are evergreen trees with thick foliage, intense colors, and fragrant flowers, used in various fields for making fruit juices, essences, jams, pastries, cosmetics and in the pharmaceutical industry. The importance of citrus fruits and the orange in particular is evident, and if you say orange, you say Sicily.

The earliest evidence of the production of the sweet orange in Sicily, as we know it today, is found in Antonio Venuto and his *De Agricultura Opusculum,* dated 1516. Sicily offers the best climatic conditions for growing the fruit—a stroke of luck that the Sicilians cherish and are rightly proud of. In particular the red orange of Sicily PGI has unique qualities, such as its color, size, and the yield in juice that makes it particularly precious. And then there are varieties such as sanguinello, tarocco, and moro, grown above all in eastern Sicily. Towns such as Paternò, Ramacca, Augusta, Regalmuto, Floridia, Comiso, and Vittoria, not to mention Bagheria in the province of Palermo, are key centers in the world production of oranges. An ideal habitat, congenial to the development and production of citrus fruits, it is an agricultural land that man has worked intensively and loved, shaping it and fostering the gifts of nature. The red earth reveals the presence of iron that, by the hard work, sacrifices, and constancy of the Sicilian farmers, has been improved—ready to produce fruits of notable quality. The climate is never too cold, with mild winds and moderate rainfall to create the right geological and climatic balance for a territory perfect for growing citrus fruits. The numbers speak for themselves. Oranges dominate the market. With over 50 percent of the total production, it is the most widely grown of Sicilian citrus fruits, followed by mandarins and lemons. Among the Italian regions, beyond Sicily, which has the highest production (over 1½ million metric tons), Calabria and Puglia rank second and third. Overall about 170,000 hectares are devoted to the cultivation of citrus fruits, while production is around 3.3 million metric tons.

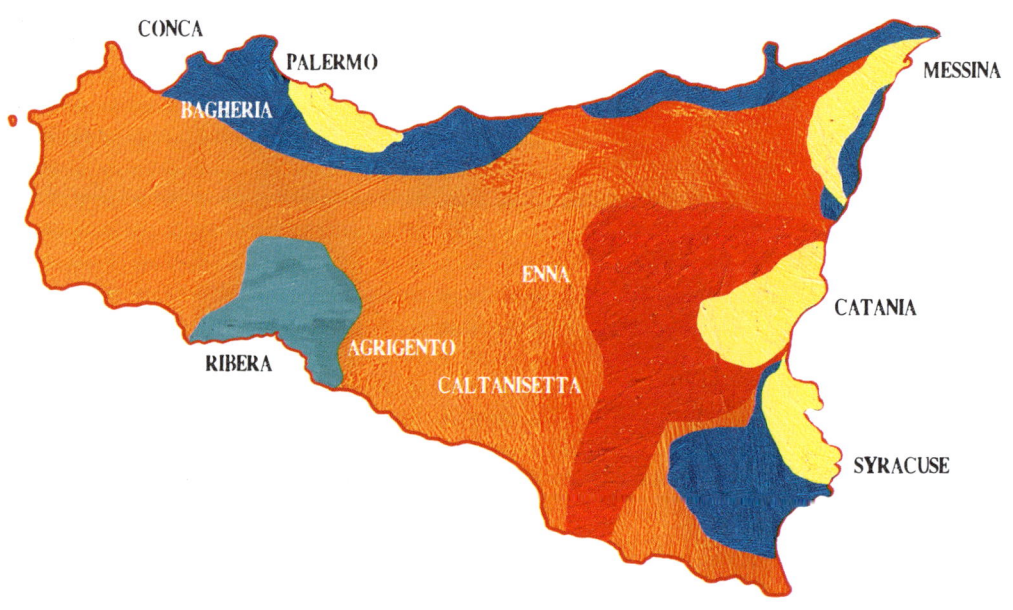

Cosmetics and Perfumes

Aestheticians in ancient Egypt were already extracting essences and perfumes from the essential oils of citrus fruits 5,000 years ago. The pharaohs and nobility set great store by the care of the body. The ritual of cleansing was performed four times a day: it entailed purifying the body and enhancing its beauty in order to approach the gods. The production of perfumes and essences was therefore crucial and gave rise to an extensive market with the creation of scented resins, perfumes for religious rites, and ointments. During the reign of **Queen Hatshepsut**, one of the few ancient Egyptian women pharaohs, "themed" trips were organized in search of plants, resins, and flowers for the preparation of new oils and ointments.

Various techniques of extraction were used: *enfleurage*, which involved arranging alternating layers of animal fat and orange blossoms on stone slabs, so exploiting the extractive and fluidifying power of fat to create delicate and refined scented essences. Another widespread method of extraction was *steam distillation*, which consisted of placing a plant on a grid connected to a coil through which passed steam at 110°C (230°F): in this way the plant released its essence, which floated on the water, ready to be used. Among the best known fragrances were the orange water and rose water adored by Queen Cleopatra. Together with roses, citrus fruits are the most widely used sources of cosmetics.

They enhance the potential of floral essences, with the citrus notes of mandarin and bergamot forming the olfactory base of almost all perfumes, creating a balanced, fresh and harmonious fragrance. It should be remembered that the bergamot in particular adds freshness and sweetness to the top notes and is used in all kinds of Eau de Cologne, like those produced by Guerlain, Hermès, Dior, and Lancôme.

The beneficial properties of citrus fruits have also been recognized at the scientific level through aromacology, the study that relates the physical and mental reactions of people to scents. Through the fragrances, reactions such as relaxation, joy, sensuousness, confidence, and happiness are triggered in direct connection with the brain's limbic system. So we can say that citrus fruit touches the nerve center of our sense of pleasure.

Among the essences produced in Sicily, the *zagara* deserves a place of honor. This is the blossom of the orange, lemon, and bergamot. These delicate and fragrant flowers are used in the preparation of floral Eau de Cologne and are most richly scented in April and May, when they are picked, processed, and mixed to form a blend of essential oils and aromas, giving rise to a fragrance with a strong Sicilian identity. This scent was known and prized by the Arabs, who heightened its aesthetic qualities and devised techniques for extracting the essential oils that are still used today. But the large-scale dissemination of perfumes and the extraction of oils from the peel of citrus fruits and the petals of orange blossom was definitely the work of Italians. The orange water produced during the Renaissance spread through Italy and delighted the Sicilian ladies of the day.

In 1610 the Bolognese philosopher and doctor Baldassarre Pisanelli wrote about orange blossom in general: "The flowers are silver in color and a water is made from them that surpasses all scents; the leaves are emerald, the fruits golden: for this reason they are called Anarantia. They are good against pestilential fevers." Eau de Cologne dates from the late 1600s. Extracted from essential oils of bergamot peel and orange blossom, it was used by the European aristocracy and given the name of "essence of neroli."

How essence of citrus was extracted in Sicily

The peel of citrus fruits contains many properties. It is an excellent ally in the kitchen for flavoring dishes, and the tiny particles of molecules are essential to cosmetics and perfumery. Many processing industries in Sicily use the peel, extracting essential oils from it. It contains cells rich in essential oil. Production of this oil is an important natural raw material for the agri-food industry, as well as the culinary and confectionery industries, being used in cosmetics and for many other commercial purposes.

The process of extracting the essence from citrus fruits dates back to the mid-19th century. The first method used was the fully manual sponge process, common until the mid-20th century. The work consisted in cutting the citrus fruit into two parts with a sharp knife. These were then hollowed out with a scoop called a *rastrello*. Then the peel was pressed manually against sea sponges. These were squeezed with a hand press and the emulsion that came out was collected in tin-lined copper containers called cunculine, where the essence, being oily, rose to the surface and was poured off into other copper containers. The most precious essence was and is that of lemon, and in particular that of Sicilian lemons, prized worldwide for its unmistakable and intense aroma.

Initially, the liquid from the fruit was not used for making juice, but delivered to two major industries that through a chemical reaction transformed it into citric acid. In this way the Chimica Arenella industrial facility was founded in Palermo as the world's largest producer of citric acid and sulfuric acid at the time, but now derelict, and in 1916 ISAC (Sicilian Citric Acid Manufacturer) in Messina.

In the decade at the turn of the century many citrus processing plants developed in Sicily, such as the **Agrumaria Corleone** (1890), now in its fourth generation, Sanderson & Sons (1895) of Tremestieri (Messina), Simone Gatto, Caminiti, and Baller in Messina. These firms long worked only on the production of essential oils, then began processing and exporting lemon juice, oranges, blood oranges, and mandarins. To all this, today's industries have added ever more advanced and reliable biological products and facilities.

Systems for obtaining essential oil

Today, the most common method for extracting the essence from citrus fruits is CP (cold pressing). The machines used for extraction include the **birillatrice**, a system with five sloping channels which feed five lemons into the mechanism. (The earliest specimens date from 1945 and were made by the Sicilian Indelicato and Speciale companies.) The lemons are cut and squeezed against rotating cylinders, and the juice extracted. The halved lemon skins fall into tanks containing a solution of water and lime, where they remain for eight hours, turning hard, and then they are conveyed to a machine called a *sfumatrice*, where they are strongly pressed in a shower of water to extract the essential oil. This method has now been superseded by more efficient equipment and systems, such as:

The **pelatrice**, also produced by the two Sicilian companies, is a machine consisting of a bed of 10-12 revolving rasping rollers, on which the fruits flow under a shower of water to capture the essential oil that escapes from the peel. The rasped fruits are moved to a roller extractor, where they are pressed for the extraction of the juice.

The **Brown-type peeler** is a machine similar to the previous one, but here the rotating rollers are replaced by a vibrating "fakir bed" with its surface covered with spikes, wholly immersed in water. The water-oil emulsion is again separated by centrifugation. The pricked fruits then go into a roller extractor where they are pressed to extract the juice.

FMC **in-line machines** compress the whole fruit between two ½ cups, one above the other, and the pressure squeezes out on **one side the essential oil** (contained in the pockets of the peel), which is carried off by a shower of water and becomes an emulsion: this is passed through a centrifuge to separate the essential oil from the water. **On the other side the juice** is squeezed out and has various uses.

Pressing is mainly used for small fruits, such as green mandarins, clementines, and small green lemons. The whole fruits are sent for processing through a continuous double-helix press that compresses them strongly, extracting a liquid that is a mixture of juice plus essential oil. This mixture is then centrifuged to separate the essential oil from the juice.

Curiosities and Information

Perhaps not everyone knows that the orange is born pointing upwards; then, as it ripens, its weight shifts the branch so that the fruit hangs from it.
The color of the orange varies according to its exposure to sunlight.

Those most exposed to cold mature first and have a stronger color and are even sweeter. We have already spoken of the varieties, which cover different ripening periods, so ensuring a broad annual production. Now we can examine them in detail.

Tarocco

One of the earliest known red flesh varities. Imported from China in 1600, the fruit is large and fragrant, the skin thin, smooth and firm. It is seedless. Its red color is due to its late ripening. Particularly prized are the oranges grown in the Catanese area, on the slopes of Etna: because of the thermal excursions, this fruit is highly sought after. It ripens in December-April and is grown mainly for consumption fresh.

Valencia

Ripens in late April, but is also harvested in June and is seedless. It has a light orange hue. The juice is very sweet, making it suitable for juicing. The presence of antioxidants makes it useful for combating tumors and cardiovascular diseases. Very common in Spain, it was used as an ornamental plant in the mosques of Cordoba and Seville. The Valencia orange is the most common variety worldwide.

Ovale

Among the most valuable varieties, is marketed from April to June. Productivity is low and uneven. The color is yellow-orange; the fruits ripen individually and in particular at the top. Grown for the table, it is also used in the preparation of desserts and savory dishes, candied and juiced. It is rich not only in Vitamins C, B1, B2, PP, flavonoids, polyphenols and antioxidant molecules, but also helps boost the immune system and combats intestinal and hepatic disorders. The areas most suitable for its production are the province of Syracuse and Calabria.

Moro

The reddest of the pigmented oranges, it has a strong, full taste. It is very aromatic and the pulp contains large amounts of juice. The peel is orange veined with various colors tending to dark red. The flesh is seedless. It is the orange with the greatest antioxidant power. It begins to ripen in early December/January. Very common in the Lentini area in the province of Syracuse.

Navelina

Ripens from October to December: as it ripens, it varies in hue from pale yellow to a deep orange; the leaves are very dark. A medium-sized tree, it is raised from micro-grafts on California rootstock. The pulp is very juicy and seedless.

Thompson

The ripening period is from February to April; it is a sunny yellow color and has a sweet taste. The shape of the fruit is oblong and it is grown mainly for the table. At the base of the orange it has a distinctive navel.

Belladonna

Also known as San Giuseppe (very common in the area of Villa San Giuseppe, in Calabria): ripens from mid-December to February-March. The peel is yellow and thick, the foliage dense and bright green; the pulp is orange and the juice yield is over 50 percent. It is very sweet thanks to the high sugar content and it is rich in Vitamin C, equivalent to over 40 milligrams per 100 ml. of juice. They are also called *tsar oranges* because Russian rulers consumed them extensively. Grown for the table.

Sanguinello

Reached Italy from Spain in the nineteenth century. The peel is orange with red traces, due to water-soluble pigments known as anthocyanins. It is ideal for juicing. Ripens from February to April.

Washington Navel

Ripening from mid-December to May: with an intense orange color, the shape is round, the leaves dark green, the flowers very fragrant and it reaches its maximum abundance in spring. The peel is very compact and the Washington Navel is noted for having inside it another small, very sweet, seedless orange. The tree can withstand temperatures of -10°C (14°F).

Femminello Lemon of Syracuse

The area of cultivation is the south-east of Sicily, in soil with exceptional fertility and abundant reserves of water. The temperate climate and the picking of the fruits by hand, make the Lemon of Syracuse PGI unique.

Cultivated within 10 km of the Ionian Sea and below 210 meters above sea level the Lemon of Syracuse PGI flourishes and bears fruit three times a year, rich in juice and citric acid. The wealth of oil-bearing glands in the peel and the high quality of its essential oils, make this a prodigy of nature, a fruit always present on our tables.

The protection and promotion of the Lemon of Syracuse PGI are entrusted to a consortium set up in 2,000 as a gamble by a small group of farmers. Today it accounts for 33 percent of the total Italian lemon production.

Late tangerine of Ciaculli

Cultivated in the Palermo district of Ciaculli, where local features lead it to ripen later than other varieties. It possesses organoleptic, antioxidant, nutritional and uniquely inimitable beneficial properties.
It ripens fully between January and March. Production covers an area about 900 hectares, of which 35 percent is organic, with about 6,000 metric tons of tangerines marketed in the most productive periods.

The characteristic landforms in the area of Ciaculli-Croceverde Giardina, amid sloping and very narrow mountain valleys, make it impossible to use modern machinery. They are therefore grown using non-invasive techniques, where human labor predominates over agricultural machines.

A single orange plant can produce 500 fruits annually. Among oranges some varieties have the distinctive feature of incorporating a "second orange." This **umbilicate** group is known as **navel oranges**.

Among the most popular oranges are the red orange of Sicily PGI, cultivated in the eastern part of the island, between the provinces of Catania, Enna and Syracuse, and the orange of Ribera DOP.

For every 100 grams, an orange has a caloric intake of 35 kcl. It also contains a significant dose of **phosphorus**, used by the body in various **brain functions**, contained in a ratio of about 22 milligrams per 100 grams of pulp. It also contains a minimal amount of sodium so it is suitable in hyposodic diets.

The most common vitamin in oranges is **Vitamin C**, followed by **Niacin** (Vitamin B12) in the ratio of 0.2 mg/100 grams, **Thiamin** (Vitamin B1) in the ratio of 0.06 mg/100 grams, and **riboflavin** (Vitamin B6) in the ratio of 0.05. **Vitamin A** (Retinol) is also present in the ratio of 71 micrograms.

Oranges do not contain cholesterol.

In general, around one billion citrus fruits are grown yearly on the planet, with world fruit production reaching 100 million metric tons. A citrus tree lives for 100 years and every year in spring it produces about 60,000 flowers (orange blossom). Of these, 1 percent will grow into fruit.

The characteristics of citrus fruits include a curious feature of grapefruit juice, which enhances the action of Viagra.

On February 8, 1895, frost destroyed almost all the orange trees in Florida and production fell by 97 percent.

In the early years of the 20th century, the *California Fruit Growers Exchange* commissioned the advertising magnate **Albert Lasker** to solve what for farmers had become an economic loss. Production of oranges outstripped demand on the domestic and foreign market, and every year large quantities were destroyed. **Albert Lasker** had a brilliant idea and turned a loss into a new opportunity, transforming a product existing in nature into a **new primary consumer good**. In a nutshell he invented the marketing of orange juice with the motto: **"Drink an orange."**

The Economy

The numbers are eloquent. Sicily produces over 1.5 million metric tons of citrus fruit yearly, and has always been the leader in the Italian market. The area of land devoted to growing oranges amounts to nearly 90,000 hectares. Oranges are the most common citrus fruit, and the Tarocco is the most abundant variety, followed by the Navel, Sanguinello, and the Washington Navel. The two graphs below show the surface area devoted to growing citrus fruits in Italy and the area in hectares in Sicily devoted to growing oranges.

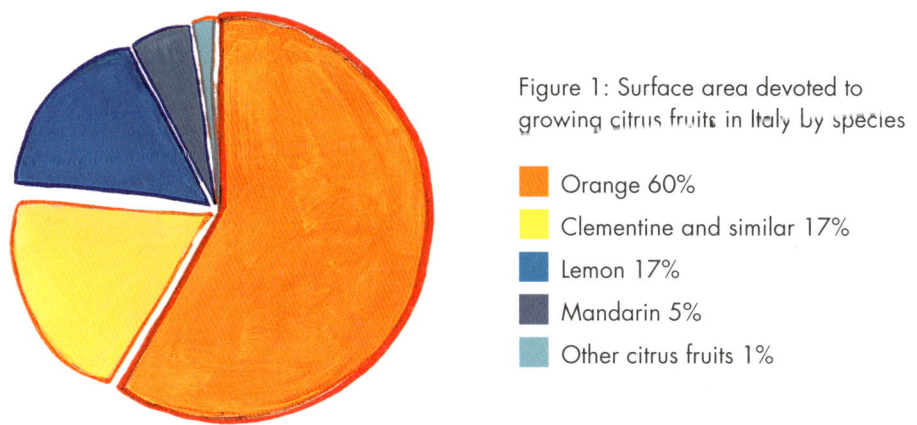

Figure 1: Surface area devoted to growing citrus fruits in Italy by species

- Orange 60%
- Clementine and similar 17%
- Lemon 17%
- Mandarin 5%
- Other citrus fruits 1%

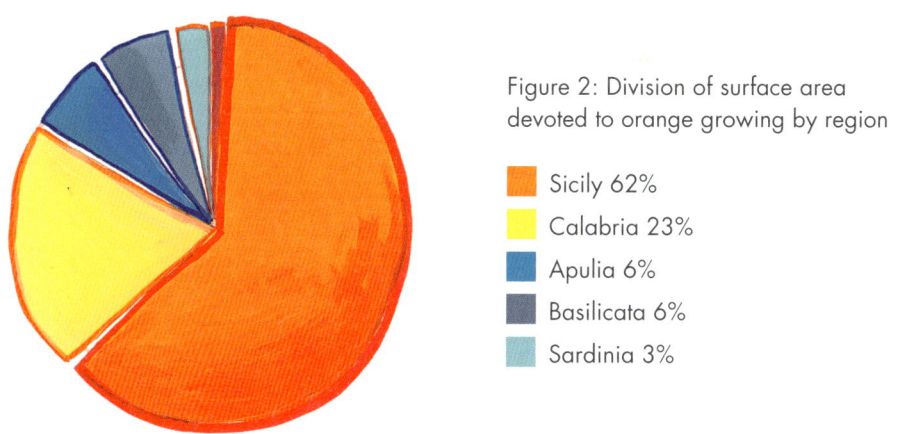

Figure 2: Division of surface area devoted to orange growing by region

- Sicily 62%
- Calabria 23%
- Apulia 6%
- Basilicata 6%
- Sardinia 3%

In Sicily, the origins of a successful economic system lie in the late 19th century. The New World appreciated oranges, and Sicilians shipped over 22,000 metric tons of citrus fruits annually to the US market. Then the Americans identified Florida as having ideal soil and climate for growing citrus fruit. In this way, the strategies changed and new markets were found, including Germany, Austria, Britain, and France. The success was immediate, with the products diversified according to market: hence there were "German" and "British" oranges, and others grown for the French market, etc., all with different characteristics.
In Europe, large quantities of peel were also in demand, being used in confectionery and cosmetics. By the late 19th century Sicily was fragrant with orange blossom. Over 8,000 hectares of land were covered with citrus groves and Sicily soon took the lead in the production and export of citrus fruits throughout the Mediterranean, also enhancing and discovering new citrus fruits and new varieties such as grapefruit, bergamot, and the Mediterranean mandarin.

The processing industries occupy a significant part of the production of citrus fruit. Today Italy produces about 60 million liters of orange juice annually to meet the demand for 500 million liters of orange juice at 12 percent of orange juice. The numbers are certain to grow because the latest European standards have raised the proportion of juice to 20 percent. Hence over 250 million kilos of blond oranges will be required to meet demand. This quantity can hardly be produced in Italy, which risks having to buy juice abroad.
Sicily meets about 50 percent of the national demand. The new European standard aims to provide the daily requirement of Vitamin C and reduce the intake of artificial coloring and flavors in beverages. All this means about 10,000 hectares more of citrus groves in Sicily, so that we can hope to see the Conca d'Oro soon reborn around Palermo.

BOSTON

NEW YORK

USA

MIAMI

1880: Beginning of cultivation of oranges in the United States.

-- 1820: Beginning of exports of Sicilian oranges to the United States and countries of northern Europe.

-- 1860: Great development of the exports to all countries. The Sicilian oranges become most widespread.

— 1910: Consolidation of exports but rapid fall in the price of oranges due to the spread of cultivation around the world: especially in Spain, Florida, California and Brazil.

Culture, Myths and Legends

The tree with its golden fruits has inspired many stories, myths, and legends that found their way into Greek mythology and are still told in the present day.

Atalanta, to please her father who wanted her to marry, promised to choose any suitor who could beat her in a running race. Hippomenes, who was deeply in love with Atalanta, hoped to win her hand and turned for help to Aphrodite, the goddess of love. She gave Hippomenes three golden apples, which he rolled before Atalanta as she ran, to distract her and enable him to win the race. As the golden apples fell to the ground, Atalanta stooped to pick them up, pausing in the race and enabling Hippomenes to overtake her: in this way he won the race and Atalanta as his bride. These "golden apples," it has been surmised, may well have been oranges. Life, we know, is made up of coincidences, sometimes even of symbols, and so the tale comes full circle! The story of the Dutch royal family is an example. The royal house of the Netherlands is called Orange-Nassau, a double surname that derives from the possessions it has held in France in the Principality of Orange since 1544. At that time, oranges were not yet grown in the area, but when they began to spread and the lands of the city of Orange were colored with orange, the link between the sovereign family of the Netherlands and the orange was indissoluble, so much so that later orange was also adopted as the color of the country's football team.

The War of Oranges between Spain and Portugal broke out in 1801, a curious and fascinating episode. Botticelli's *La Primavera* was painted to celebrate the marriage of Lorenzo di Pierfrancesco to Semiramide Appiani. Orange trees appear, framing the mythological scene. The painting is celebrated. The scene that appears to our eyes is a grove of orange trees with the ground spangled with flowers, where nine figures move in small groups, including Cupid fluttering high above Venus. All Renaissance art is rich in symbolism drawing on the white orange blossom (a symbol of chastity) and the fruit as a symbol of fertility and much else. In literature, Nicolò Speciale, a 14th-century historian, in *De Siculis rebus*, described the bitter oranges produced by "trees with sour fruits." Antonino Venuto da Noto (?-1550) in the *De agricultura opusculum*, written in 1510 and published in Naples in 1516, subdivided citrus fruits into four species ("Orange, Citron, Lemon, and Bergamot"). He refers explicitly to sweet oranges in his first chapter, which begins with this challenging statement: "The orange is clearly the King, Prince and Lord of all trees." Among the most fascinating and complete works we cannot fail to mention *Hesperides, sive De Malorum aureorum Cultura et Usu Libri Quatuor*, a monograph packed with information, which combines the charm of mythology and legends, a fundamental and pioneering work of literature on citrus fruits.

For centuries in the Carnival tradition, oranges were emblematic of opulence and amusement. There was the well-known custom of holding mock battles in which oranges were used as projectiles, flung violently between rival teams traveling in carts. The battles became so fierce that metal shutters had to be fitted to the windows of houses to prevent them from being broken. At the carnival of Ivrea in Piedmont every year on Sunday and Monday of Carnival week and Shrove Tuesday, the spectacular battle of the oranges is still fought, a tradition that has its roots in the Middle Ages, with teams of *Aranceri* defending their quarter of the city by hurling oranges at their rivals.

Oranges were also a symbol of libertinage and immorality. In Elizabethan times, the boisterous and buxom orange vendors offered their graces as well as oranges to the powerful, aspiring to receive a career at court by their attractions. At the Restoration, Charles II saw Nell Gwynn selling oranges in the theater and made her his mistress. This fostered the collective image of orange sellers as women willing to do anything to raise their social status. Greek mythology relates that Juno, when she married Jupiter, brought as her dowry some small trees with golden fruits, symbols of fruitfulness and love. For fear that thieves would steal this precious gift, Jupiter kept them in a garden where they were guarded by the nymphs of the Hesperides, maidens famed for their sweet singing. Again drawing on Greek mythology, we read that the eleventh of the labors of Hercules required him to steal the fruit of the Hesperides by defeating the dragon that Juno had also placed to defend the garden. In Norwegian mythology, the gods were threatened by old age, but by eating the "golden apples" they kept their youth forever. The goddess Idun was the guardian of the garden where the golden-skinned fruit grew. With the passing of time, in Norway, there there grew the custom of annually electing the Queen of the Oranges, who represents sensuousness, nature, and strength.

Health and Gastronomy

The wealth of antioxidants in oranges and citrus fruits in general and their genetic qualities contribute in fundamental ways to our well-being. This is crucial to enable us to understand, appreciate, and evaluate the orange as the fruit that has most to offer in terms of health and general well-being.

Fresh, tasty, juicy, and invigorating, the orange is a genuine, simple, and natural supplement, ensuring an immediate supply of energy to the body, as well as heightening the functions of the immune system, reducing signs of aging, increasing cell repair and metabolism, detoxifying the body, improving circulation, moderating blood pressure, reducing inflammation, and lowering cholesterol levels.

The orange also offers the advantage that it can be eaten whole, including the peel, provided it has no additives or added sugars. So a fruit that is 100 percent organic is like a small sun concentrated in your hands ready to give you an extra charge, a natural snack of unique vitality and always available.

This is a fruit that is found in Sicily at every street corner, in the markets of Palermo like those of Catania, Ragusa, Syracuse, and many other towns. In spring the island becomes a white cloud of orange blossom. The heady scent spreads through the air and the first heat warms hearts and minds. The gardens are filled with oranges, lemons, and mandarins. In their hands brides hold a small bouquet of orange flowers: clasping it, with its festive overtones, they dream and love! At Easter, every year at **Terrasini** in the province of Palermo the "Festa di li schietti" is held. Tradition has it that the young *schietti* (bachelors) have to conquer their beloved's heart by showing their skill and strength by lifting an orange tree weighing over 50 kilos before their fiancée, balancing it and spinning it. The festival dates from far in the past (it has been recorded since the early 19th century), and every year it attracts thousands of people. The tree with the golden fruit strikes again!

Your desire for oranges and citrus fruits will soon be satisfied with 30 specially composed recipes, simple yet refined dishes, some innovative and others reflecting Sicilian traditions. You will have the opportunity to win a place in the hearts of your guests after they have tasted your recipes. Step by step, we will give you all the information needed to recreate on your table the flavors you will have imagined in reading this book.

We will bring the tastes and colors of Sicily to your table: a culinary journey to discover new dishes, from the art of Sicilian pastry to the gastronomic tradition, while dreaming of the warm sun on the largest island in the Mediterranean.

So indulge yourself and browse the pages in search of the perfect recipe that best represents you. Spoil yourself with our cuisine scented with citrus fruits and fantasy.

The Taste of Orange

Move and the Earth will move with you, tracing your life, following and controlling it, and your path will be certain. Color your dreams orange and the days will smile on you and purify you. Citrus fruits, oranges in particular, move the world of dreams, hopes, health, summer, and well-being. When life is orange-scented, then everything is fine and nothing is wrong. Time flies without your noticing it, like music, like a rhythm that touches you and whispers: "oranges bring us together and make us feel fine." So let's get together and feel alright!

Put it in salads, eat it naturally, squeeze it and drink it immediately! Quench your thirst and drink some more, and then peel it, but do not throw away the peel! Take the orange cut into slices and season it as you like, as we will soon be doing with 30 fresh recipes, unique and imaginative but especially easy to prepare. Remembering that easy does not mean simple, we will make the recipes stellar but feasible.

And if we talk of oranges, we will also talk of citrus fruits. Whoever saw a sad lemon? All lemons are happy, bright, and ready to radiate and cheer up the grumpy side of your character. Citrus fruits and happiness are an indissoluble union and create positive energy. Your life is a big carton of oranges waiting to be unwrapped.
As Vincent Van Gogh said: There is no blue without yellow and without orange, and if you add blue, you must also add yellow and orange.

And does your life taste of orange?
Enjoy the recipes, which offer something for everyone!

Dishes & Salads

Octopus salad with sweet and sour apples, oranges, and celery p. 69
Bread salad with smoked herring and warm citrus dressing p. 71
Whole-wheat flour pasta with a miscellany of seafood, oranges, and radishes p. 72
Couscous with dates, pomegranate, coconut and pineapple, reduced vinegar, honey, and oranges p. 74
Venus rice with yellow cherry tomatoes, shrimp, cashews in citrus emulsion, with crispy rice puffs and caper berries p. 76
Steamed flaked cod with orange slices p. 80
Diversification of legumes with celery hearts, sultanas, oranges, sweet and sour onion p. 82
Tuna and salad, garnished with orange wedges, octopus, and cuttlefish p. 86
Salad with "fregula," soncino, smoked dorado, spring onions, tomatoes, and oranges p. 90
Grilled cheese medallions cooked and flavored with orange, garnished with salad leaves and mandarins p. 92
Beef salad marinated in cumin with orange gelatin p. 94
Triumph of vegetables and fillets of orange peel in syrup p. 98
Potatoes with orange yogurt dressing and chives. Fillets of beef marinated and pineapple squares with candied apricots p. 100
Mixture of citrus fruits with red onion, green olives, fennel, and caciocavallo crusts p. 102
Fragrant field vegetables with dried fruit, chicken, wafers of caciocavallo, and crispy bacon p. 106
Roulades of sardines and scabbardfish p. 108
Swordfish parcel flavored with citrus fruits p. 110
Duck breast with Sicilian citrus and rabbit terrine p. 112

Dishes & Salads

Octopus salad with sweet and sour apples, oranges, and celery

With all the flavors of the sea heightened by oranges, this salad merits a place in the list of your favorite dishes and on the table of all those who love the richness of sea and land in Sicily.

—

Ingredients for the "land of lemon and shrimp":
66 g (2.3 oz) unsalted butter
35 g (1.2 oz) shrimp flesh passed through a sieve
A pinch of salt
4 g (1 tsp) sugar
30 g (1.1 oz) grated primosale cheese
90 g (3.2 oz) almond flour
44 g (1.6 oz) plain flour
2 yolks of hardboiled eggs passed through a sieve

Ingredients for the salad:
100 g (3.5 oz) sugar
75 g (2.6 oz) vinegar
8 segments of orange
2.6 g ($^2/_4$ tsp) grated lemon zest
Basil leaves to taste
1 bay leaf
120 g (4.2 oz) celery diced and blanched in water and vinegar
180 g (6.3 oz) boiled green and white beans
16 g (0.5 oz) capers
4 spring peas in their pods
280 g (10 oz) boiled octopus
1 Golden Delicious apple
4 slices dehydrated lemon
Salt to taste

Dishes & Salads

Method for the "land of lemon and shrimp":
Knead the butter together with the shrimp flesh, egg boiled and sieved, salt, sugar and grated primosale. Finally add the different kinds of flour. Roll out the dough, cook at 140°C (285°F), cool and crumble them as if they were clods of earth.

Method for the salad:
Make a sweet and sour dressing with vinegar, sugar and a bay leaf. When it starts to simmer, add the orange slices, grated lemon zest and basil, filter and cool. Place the sweet and sour celery on the dish with the capers and the octopus. Serve with small pieces of boiled green and white beans, spring peas in their pods (do not eat the pods), segments of orange, slices of apple, the dehydrated slice of lemon and the "land of lemon and shrimp."

Octopus salad with sweet and sour apples, oranges, and celery

Dishes & Salads

Bread salad with smoked herring and warm citrus dressing

A simple and fascinating bread salad with herring and citrus dressing, an original and delicious combination.

—

Ingredients for dressing of orange-flavored extra virgin olive oil:
45 g (1.6 oz) extra virgin olive oil
Peel of a grated orange
1 g (¼ tsp) fresh marjoram
Salt to taste

Ingredients for salads:
400 g (14 oz) bread made from durum wheat semolina
Salad leaves and aromatic herbs to taste
100 g (3.5 oz) smoked herring
35 g (1.2 oz) julienned red onion
60 g (2.1 oz) julienned carrots
Segments of oranges and mandarins to taste

—

Method for dressing of orange-flavored extra virgin olive oil:
Heat the ingredients and serve.

Composition:
Place some toasted squares of bread on a plate, add a few baby salad leaves, herring fillets, julienned red onion and carrots, segments of mandarins and oranges. Season with the extra virgin olive oil flavored with oranges, salt and marjoram.

Dishes & Salads

Whole-wheat flour pasta with a miscellany of seafood, oranges, and radishes

Dedicated to those who love taste and refinement and are bold, this dish will challenge even the most sophisticated palate.

—

Ingredients for the pasta:
200 g (7 oz) whole wheat pasta
80 g (2.8 oz) shelled mussels
80 g (2.8 oz) shelled clams
80 g (2.8 oz) shelled shrimp
80 g (2.8 oz) julienned squid
80 g (2.8 oz) boiled octopus
25 g (1 oz) extra virgin olive oil
25 g (1 oz) lemon juice
15 g ($2/4$ oz) orange juice
3 g ($2/3$ tsp) parsley
1 sliced radish
8 segments of an orange

—

Simmer the pasta, cool in cold water and salt, drain and season with the ingredients described above and previously cooked. Season with oil, lemon juice and oranges. Before serving add the parsley to the leaves, sliced radish and segments of orange.

Place the pasta with the seafood on the plate, enrich with the orange segments, the radishes previously marinated and parsley.

Dishes & Salads

Couscous with dates, pomegranate, coconut and pineapple, reduced vinegar, honey, and oranges

A dish definitely characterized by strong Mediterranean flavors, with high nutritional values and many beneficial properties, starting from the honey and the health-giving dates.

—

Ingredients:
280 g (10 oz) precooked couscous, revived and cooked in vegetable stock
60 g (2.1 oz) vinegar
40 g (1.4 oz) honey
70 g (2.5 oz) coconut flakes
80 g (2.8 oz) ripe pomegranate
120 g (4.2 oz) pineapple

Mint leaves to taste
12 dates
Orange segments or oranges in syrup to taste
6 g (1¼ tsp) grated orange peel
40 g (1.4 oz) sugar
35 g (1.2 oz) extra virgin olive oil
Salt to taste

—

Cook the couscous in vegetable stock, cool and then season with the reduced vinegar with honey, flaked coconut, pomegranate, diced pineapple and mint leaves. Garnish with pitted dates and orange slices, fillets of oranges, grated orange peel, sugar, oil and salt.

Preparation for the vinegar reduction:

Bring vinegar and honey to a boil, stir until completely melted, and continue to cook until the dressing has reduced its volume to about half.

Dishes & Salads

Venus rice with yellow cherry tomatoes, shrimp, cashews in citrus emulsion, with crispy rice puffs and caper berries

One of the most popular varieties of rice, it will triumph on your table, regaling your guests with unexpected delights and the surprising flavors of Sicilian cuisine.

—

Method for the rice:
Simmer the rice, cool it and, at serving, compose the dish by adding the tomatoes peeled and cut into wedges, the unshelled shrimps and orange slices. Season with the emulsion of extra virgin olive oil, orange and lemon juice, a pinch of salt, cashews, caper berries and lemon rice puffs.

Method for the crispy rice puffs:
Cook the rice until it is well done. When almost cooked, add the grated lemon peel. Pour and cool. Pass it all through the cutter and then through a sieve. Spread a thin layer of the rice mixture on oven paper and dehydrate it in a static oven at 65°C (150°F) or cook it in the microwave taking care it does not burn.

Dishes & Salads

Ingredients for the rice:
240 g (8.5 oz) venus rice
175 g (6.2 oz) yellow cherry tomatoes
480 g (17 oz) frozen and shelled red shrimp suitable to be eaten raw in keeping with the health rules
40 g (1.4 oz) extra virgin olive oil
25 g (1 oz) lemon juice
25 g (1 oz) orange juice
Salt to taste
40 g (1.4 oz) salted cashew nuts
Caper berries to taste
Orange slices

Ingredients for the rice puffs:
60 g (2.1 oz) riso originario for the boiled meat
Grated zest of a lemon
Salt to taste

Dishes & Salads
Steamed flaked cod with orange slices

Ingredients:
400 g (14 oz) fillet of cod
Arugula as required
1 orange divided into segments

For the dressing:
40 g (1.4 oz) extra virgin olive oil
50 g (1.8 oz) strawberries
3 g (2/3 tsp) lesser calamint
½ clove black garlic
3 g (2/3 tsp) chives
12 g (0.4 oz) red vinegar

1 slice of dehydrated orange

Dishes & Salads

A very light, sophisticated and refined salad with chic and irreverent overtones, a reinterpretation of cod with a strong flavor, which will challenge even the most brazen palates.

—

Steam or simmer the cod, cool and flake the flesh.

Trim and clean the arugula. Put in a plate with the orange slices.
Separately, place strawberries, calamint, extra virgin olive oil, red vinegar,
½ clove of black garlic and chives in a siphon.

Load the siphon and set aside. Before serving, carefully work the siphon without upturning it and let the gas out. After all the gas has left the siphon,
open it and serve the dressing.

Garnish with a slice of dehydrated orange.

Dishes & Salads

Diversification of legumes with celery hearts, sultanas, oranges, and sweet and sour onion

A luxuriant salad with a thousand facets. You will be surprised by the combinations of flavors, from the celery heart to the sweet-and-sour onion, all enriched by the orange juice and slices.

—

Ingredients:
280 g (10 oz) mixed boiled vegetables
60 g (2.1 oz) julienned of carrots
90 g (3.2 oz) orange segments
40 g (1.4 oz) dried fruit
80 g (2.8 oz) sweet and sour onion
40 g (1.4 oz) extra virgin olive oil
30 g (1.1 oz) orange juice

Salt to taste
40 g (1.4 oz) sultanas revived in orange juice
90 g (3.2 oz) semi-mature caciocavallo
16 mint leaves
30 g (1.1 oz) lemon juice
Fillets of citrus fruit in syrup to taste
1 slice of dehydrated red onion

—

Mix the various legumes, enriching the dish with the julienned carrots, segments of orange, dried fruit, the julienned sweet and sour onion and the emulsion of extra virgin olive oil with orange juice, lemon juice, fillets of citrus fruit and salt.

Finish with the raisins, pieces of caciocavallo and mint leaves. In the middle of the dish, add a slice of dehydrated red onion.

Dishes & Salads

Tuna and salad, garnished with orange wedges, octopus, and cuttlefish

Ingredients for the marinated tuna:
400 g (14 oz) frozen tuna suitable for eating raw under the current health rules
1 l (1 US quart) water
78 g (2.8 oz) salt
7 g ($1^{2}/_{5}$ tbs) fresh leaves of calamint

Cuttlefish-ink gelatin:
200 ml (¾ cup) water
6 g (1¼ tsp) fish glue
1.5 g (¼ tsp) salt
Zest of grated orange
Chopped chives to taste
1 cuttlefish ink sac

Gelatin with fish stock for octopus carpaccio:
200 g (7 oz) fish stock
6 g (1¼ tsp) isinglass
1.5 g (¼ tsp) salt
Zest of a grated lemon

Ingredients for octopus and cuttlefish in gelatin:
1 octopus weighing about 1 kg (2 lb)
2 cuttlefish weighing 50 g (1.8 oz) each
Salt to taste

For the octopus 200 g (7 oz) fish stock gelatin
For the cuttlefish 200 g (7 oz) squid ink gelatin

For the salted almonds:
70 g (2.5 oz) of almond leaves
Salt to taste
Water to taste

For the dressing of extra virgin olive oil with calamint:
35 g (1.2 oz) extra virgin olive oil
7 g ($1^{2}/_{5}$ tbs) leaves of lesser calamint
8 g ($1^{2}/_{4}$ tsp) chives
1 bay leaf
1 clove garlic
35 g (1.2 oz) red vinegar
2 semi-salted anchovies
Salt to taste

Dishes & Salads

A fresh, summery dish, recalling your holiday in Sicily or encouraging you to set off at once. The recipe consists of marinated and scalded tuna, carpaccio of octopus and cuttlefish garnished with salad in season and oranges in a dressing of extra virgin olive oil and calamint.

–

For the marinated tuna:
In a saucepan, simmer the water, salt and calamint. Allow to cool.
With the tuna create strands of about 6 cm (2.3 in) in diameter, immerse them in the brine, seal the container and keep refrigerated for about 13 hours.

Next, remove the tuna from the brine, dry, and lightly sauté in a pan with extra virgin olive oil. Allow to cool and cut up.

For the cuttlefish ink gelatin:
Simmer 200 ml (¾ cup) of water, adding the cuttlefish ink sacs and salt, then cool to a temperature of 30°C (86°F), add the gelatin previously rehydrated and melted in the microwave, add the finely chopped beetroot and grated lemon zest. Serve cold.

For the gelatin for the octopus carpaccio:
Simmer the fish stock, adjust for salt, cool to a temperature of 30°C (86°F), add the gelatin previously rehydrated and dissolved in the microwave, and add the grated lemon peel. Serve cold.

Dishes & Salads

...meanwhile prepare the octopus and cuttlefish in gelatin:
Clean the cuttlefish, removing the ink sacs completely. Simmer the cuttlefish, julienne it and place it on rectangular stainless steel boxes, press it down and pour in the squid ink and allow to cool.

Apart, simmer the octopus. When it is done, place it still hot in a rectangular stainless steel container, press and pour in the fish stock gelatin.

For the salted almonds:
Moisten the almonds with water, add a little salt, mix and toast to 140°C (285°F) in the oven.

For the dressing of extra virgin olive oil and calamint:
Put all the ingredients together and heat. As soon as it is ready, cool and keep in the fridge.

Composition of the dish:
Place the salad vegetables in season and the diced tuna on the strips of carpaccio of octopus and cuttlefish in gelatin. Serve with slices of orange, salted flaked almond and calamint leaves, and season with the dressing.

Tuna and salad, garnished with orange wedges, octopus, and cuttlefish

Dishes & Salads

Salad with "fregula," soncino, smoked dorado, spring onions, tomatoes, and oranges

Sicily meets Sardinia in this salad of the two islands! The chef's touch? Ginger and kumquat … and much more.

—

Simmer the dorado, allow to cool and mix with the juice and pulp of the orange, extra virgin olive oil, garlic clove and salt.

Place the dorado on the plate, garnish with the lamb's lettuce, the previously marinated shallot, the sliced candied ginger and salted pumpkin seeds.

Finish the dish by placing the smoked dorado fillets and kumquat slices.

Garnish with a curried wafer of caciocavallo.

Dishes & Salads

Ingredients:
280 g (10 oz) dorado toasted and boiled
50 g (1.8 oz) orange juice
35 g (1.2 oz) minced orange pulp
40 g (1.4 oz) extra virgin olive oil
1 clove garlic
Salt to taste
Lamb's lettuce to taste
1 shallot marinated with water and vinegar
8 g ($1^2/4$) small pieces of candied ginger
7 g ($1^2/5$ tbs) dried and salted pumpkin seeds
Slices of kumquat to taste
240 g (8.5 oz) smoked dorado
A curried wafer of caciocavallo

Dishes & Salads

Grilled cheese medallions cooked and flavored with orange, garnished with salad leaves and mandarins

To serve as a side dish or starter, a versatile and intriguing delicacy that goes well with any course.

—

Chop all the cheeses finely. Knead them together, add the aromatic herbs and roll them out with the cheeses into a rope. Wrap in oven paper and cook. Bake in a steam oven at 75°C (167°F) for 40 minutes. Allow to cool and cut into medallions.

Place the salad with the mandarin and orange segments on a dish together with the grated citrus zest and grilled cheese medallions.

Finish with a drizzle of extra virgin olive oil, fried basil leaves and julienned tomato fried in a pan with a clove of garlic.

Dishes & Salads

Ingredients:
150 g (5.3 oz) fresh caciocavallo cheese
150 g (5.3 oz) primosale cheese
150 g (5.3 oz) tuma cheese
150 g (5.3 oz) provola dolce cheese
9 g ($1^{4}/_{5}$ tsp) chives
45 g (1.6 oz) wild fennel
30 g (1.1 oz) grated tangerine
and orange zest
Orange and mandarin segments to taste
160 g (5.6 oz) fresh tomatoes
Extra virgin olive oil to taste
Fried basil leaves to taste
1 clove garlic

Dishes & Salads

Beef salad marinated in cumin with orange gelatin

Ingredients for marinated cumin beef:
400 g (14 oz) beef tenderloin
1 g (¼ tsp) cumin
1 g (¼ tsp) chives
1 g (¼ tsp) lemon peel
1 g (¼ tsp) rosemary
60 g (2.1 oz) salt
40 g (1.4 oz) sugar

Ingredients for the orange gelatin:
200 g (7 oz) orange juice
4 g (1 tsp) grated orange zest
6 g (1 ¼ tsp) isinglass

Ingredients for the yogurt dressing with onion and cucumber:
160 g (5.6 oz) yogurt
4 g (1 tsp) chives
4 g (1 tsp) chopped cucumber
23 g (0.8 oz) orange juice
Salt to taste

Ingredients for the popcorn with rosemary:
40 g (1.4 oz) corn for popping
3 g (²/₃ tsp) fresh rosemary
Salt to taste

Dishes & Salads

A salad rich in full-bodied ingredients and clearly defined flavors, varying with every mouthful, little discoveries that will make it your favorite dish.

—

Method for the beef tenderloin:
Mix the salt with the sugar and chopped herbs. Cover the tenderloin with the marinade and place in the fridge for a couple of hours. Remove the tenderloin from the salt and cut into cubes.

Method for the gelatin:
Combine the orange juice with the zest, mix with the previously soaked fish glue and melt it in the microwave, shape the dish and place it in the fridge. Dice before serving.

Method for the yogurt dressing:
Add the chives and chopped cucumber to the yogurt and adjust for salt.
Before serving add the orange juice.

Method for the popcorn with rosemary:
Put the corn mixed with the rosemary and the salt in a container suitable for use in the microwave oven. As soon as all the corn has popped, put it in a moisture-free container.

Composition:
Finely chop the fennel and chill it in a water and ice bath. Drain and make a salad of the fennel with the young spinach leaves. Spread over the beef and the diced orange gelatin, the yogurt dressing with the feathery fennel leaves and popcorn flavored with rosemary.

Dishes & Salads

Triumph of vegetables and fillets of orange peel in syrup

Ingredients for the Triumph of vegetables:
200 g (7 oz) zucchini
200 g (7 oz) carrots
200 g (7 oz) bell peppers
200 g (7 oz) white celery
20 g (0.7 oz) basil
60 g (2.1 oz) extra virgin olive oil
18 g (0.6 oz) vinegar
60 g (2.1 oz) semi-mature caciocavallo
Orange and mandarin slices
0,5 g (1/5 tsp) fresh ginger
Salt to taste

For the orange peel in syrup:
Julienned orange peel to taste
100 g (3.5 oz) sugar
40 g (1.4 oz) water
40 g (1.4 oz) glucose
1 g (¼ tsp) cardamom

Dishes & Salads

A salad rich in full-bodied ingredients and clearly defined flavors, changing with every mouthful into the flavors of caciocavallo with red turnip.

—

Method for the vegetables:
Trim and cut the vegetables for the final composition. Before serving, the ingredients must be marinated 35 minutes in a mixture of extra virgin olive oil, vinegar, salt, basil and fresh ginger.

Method for the orange peel:
Simmer the sugar in water and glucose at a temperature of up to 104°C (220°F). Remove the syrup from the heat, add the julienned orange and cardamom. Allow to cool.

Composition:
Alternate the vegetables on the plate, add the julienned red turnip, semi-mature caciocavallo, orange and mandarin slices, pieces of semolina bread and orange zest in orange syrup. Serve with a little extra virgin olive oil.

Dishes & Salads

Potatoes with orange yogurt dressing and chives. Fillets of beef marinated and pineapple squares with candied apricots

A simple, tasty recipe, enriched with apricot and orange pineapple.
A festive dish to delight your palate.

—

Simmer the potatoes in water, salt and vinegar until they are *al dente*.

Prepare the yogurt dressing by mixing the chives, the juice and the orange pulp, the cucumber puree and a pinch of salt.

Place the salads and diced potatoes on the plate, arrange the marinated smoked meat fillets and season with the extra virgin olive oil. Finish the dish by adding the diced fresh pineapple, the candied apricots, yogurt dressing, julienne the lemon and orange zest, lemon wedges and a wafer of caciocavallo cheese.

Preparation for the fresh cacciocavallo wafer:
Place small piles of grated fresh caciocavallo on parchment paper and press with a spoon, forming small discs. Microwave until the cheese melts.
Allow to cool and serve as a garnish.

Dishes & Salads

Ingredients:
180 g (6.3 oz) potatoes cut into cubes
120 g (4.2 oz) low-fat yogurt
6 g (1 ¼ tsp) chives
25 g (1 oz) orange juice and orange pulp
16 g (0.5 oz) cucumber puree
Salt to taste
Mixed salad to taste
240 g (8.5 oz) marinated smoked beef
Extra virgin olive oil
80 g (2.8 oz) diced pineapple
40 g (1.4 oz) candied apricots
Lemon wedges to taste
Julienne the lemon and orange zest in syrup

For the fresh caciocavallo wafer:
Grated fresh caciocavallo as desired

Dishes & Salads

Mixture of citrus fruits with red onion, green olives, fennel, and caciocavallo crusts

Ingredients for the citrus gelatin:
200 g (7 oz) of equal amounts of orange, lemon and Mandarin juice
4 g (1 tsp) grated citrus peel
6 g (1¼ tsp) isinglass

Ingredients for the caciocavallo crusts:
160 g (5.6 oz) semi-mature caciocavallo diced
Dehydrated garlic to taste

Ingredients for the extra virgin olive oil flavored with mint:
150 g (5.3 oz) extra virgin olive oil
20 g (0.7 oz) lesser calamint leaves

Ingredients for the salad:
3 mandarins
2 lemons
3 oranges
200 g (7 oz) red onion
70 g (2.5 oz) green olives
240 g (8.5 oz) julienned fennel
4 radishes
Mixed salad to taste
Salt to taste

Dishes & Salads

A typical Sicilian side dish, fresh and colorful, appetizing and refined and the essence of simplicity.

—

Method for the citrus gelatin:
Combine the juice of the citrus fruit with some zest, mix it with the previously soaked gelatin and dissolve it in the microwave, shape it and place it in the fridge.
Cut into cubes before serving.

Method for the caciocavallo crusts:
Dice the caciocavallo crusts, sprinkle with dehydrated garlic, place in silicone molds for food and cook in the microwave. As soon as the cheese melts, remove the shapes and try to model them to look like small rocks.

Method for the extra virgin olive oil with mint:
Mix the oil in a container with the calamint, cover and allow to stand for 30 minutes.

Method for the salad:
Peel and arrange the citrus segments on the plate, enrich the dish with salad vegetables, dehydrated red onion, pitted green olives and julienned fennel.
Garnish with caciocavallo crusts and citrus gelatin cubes.
Before serving add a little extra virgin olive oil to the mint, sliced radishes and a pinch of salt.

Dishes & Salads

Fragrant field vegetables with dried fruit, chicken, wafers of caciocavallo, and crispy bacon

A witty and attractive recipe to amaze your friends: the variety of ingredients will make it a certain success.

—

Method for the "turmeric puff":
Whip the eggs with the sugar and salt, add the flour sifted with turmeric, pour into cardboard beakers for use with food (such as drinks beakers), cook in the microwave, cool and serve.

Method for the salad:
Simmer the chicken and cool. Cut the chicken into fillets and season with the extra virgin olive oil with rosemary, salt and balsamic vinegar. Garnish with toasted dried fruit, caciocavallo wafers, crispy bacon previously cooked at 170°C (338°F) in the oven. Serve with small pieces of "turmeric puff."

Dishes & Salads

Ingredinets for the "turmeric puff":
190 g (6.7 oz) whole eggs
35 g (1.2 oz) egg yolks
15 g (2/4 oz) sugar
1.5 g (¼ tsp) salt
128 g plain flour
1 g (¼ tsp) turmeric

Ingredients for the salad:
480 g (17 oz) chicken breast
40 g (1.4 oz) extra virgin olive oil
Rosemary
Salt to taste
15 g (2/4 oz) balsamic vinegar
100 g (3.5 oz) mixed nuts (hazelnuts, almonds, walnuts)
40 g (1.4 oz) grated caciocavallo cheese
4 slices bacon
1 orange wedges
Mixed baby salad leaves to taste

Dishes & Salads

Roulades of sardines and scabbardfish

A recipe to the traditional Sicilian dish with raisins, pine nuts, and a delicious sweet-and-sour dressing of oranges and lemons accompanied by fried scabbardfish scented with lemon thyme.

—

Ingredients for the sardine roulades:
8 sardines butterflied and boned
100 g (3.5 oz) durum wheat semolina
7 g (1 2/5 tbs) toasted pine nuts
7 g (1 2/5 tbs) raisins
3 basil leaves
12 g (0.4 oz) shallots
1 anchovy in oil
30 g (1.1 oz) extra virgin olive oil
4 slices of orange cut in half
45 g (1.6 oz) orange juice
35 g (1.2 oz) lemon juice
15 g (2/4 oz) citrus honey
30 g (1.1 oz) sugar
Salt to taste

For the sweet-and-sour dressing of red onion, olives, capers and celery scented with lemon thyme:
120 g (4.2 oz) red onion
40 g (1.4 oz) pitted olives
70 g (2.5 oz) celery
10 g (0.35 oz) capers flowers or fruits
35 g (1.2 oz) sugar
10 g (0.35 oz) white vinegar
1 g (¼ tsp) lemon thyme
Peel of grated orange
Salt to taste.

For the fried scabbardfish fillets:
240 g (8.5 oz) scabbardfish fillets
Durum wheat semolina as needed
Salt to taste
Extra virgin olive oil

Garnish of dehydrated orange:
4 slices of an orange (not too large)

Dishes & Salads

For the roulades:
Grate the bread, add the shallot previously parched in extra virgin olive oil together with the anchovy, add the basil, pine nuts, raisins, half the orange juice and salt to taste. Knead everything together and fill the boned sardines to create small roulades. Cut the slices of orange in half, place them in an oiled pan and add a sardine roll on each of the slices. Drizzle extra virgin olive oil over the sardine roulades. Bake them at 165°C (330°F). About 2–3 minutes before they are cooked, pour over the mixture of orange juice, lemon, honey and sugar. Once cooked, leave to cool.

For the sweet-and-sour dressing of red onion, olives, capers and celery scented with lemon thyme:
Julienne the onion, celery and olives. Blanch the celery, olives and capers, simmer the onion, chill it in lemon water and salt. In a small saucepan, cook the sugar and vinegar in a small pan, remove from the heat and add the grated orange zest and the lemon thyme. Leave it to cool and mix it with the ingredients previously blanched.

For the dehydrated orange garnish:
Wash and dry the orange, cut the slices very thin, place in a baking pan on a sheet of baking paper and cook in a ventilated oven at 55°C (130°F) until the orange slices are completely dehydrated.

Composition:
Place the roulades on the plate accompanying everything with some salad leaves.

Cut the scabbardfish fillets into lozenges and flour them in the durum wheat semolina, then fry them in extra virgin olive oil. Top them with the sweet-and-sour dressing of red onion, olives, capers and celery in scented lemon thyme.

Before serving, garnish each dish with a slice of dehydrated orange and a caper fruit.

Dishes & Salads

Swordfish parcel flavored with citrus fruits

Ingredients for the parcel:
600 g (21 oz) swordfish (4 slices, thick not wide)
100 g (3.5 oz) milk bread
16 g (0.5 oz) orange juice
12 g (0.4 oz) lemon juice
1.3 g (¼ tsp) grated orange zest and lemon
3.2 g (²/₃ tsp) chives
Marjoram
85 g (3 oz) boned sardines
35 g (1.2 oz) extra virgin olive oil
40 g (1.4 oz) grated primosale cheese
25 g (1 oz) white wine
Salt to taste

Ingredients for the garnish of mushrooms, carrots and sun-dried tomatoes with chives:
160 g (5.6 oz) of field mushrooms, cleaned
70 g (2.5 oz) carrots julienned
40 g (1.4 oz) scalded and peeled tomatoes
6 g (1¼ tsp) chopped chives
25 g (1 oz) extra virgin olive oil
Salt to taste

Ingredients for the ricotta and cream mousse:
100 g (3.5 oz) pasteurized sheep's milk ricotta
65 g (2.3 oz) pasteurized fresh cream with 35% fat
Salt to taste

Dishes & Salads

A delicious dish with an irresistible aroma. The colors and fragrance immediately evoke the Sicilian atmosphere of bittersweet enchantment.

—

For the parcel:
Trim the slices of swordfish and cut them into medallions. Create pockets in each slice. In a separate container put the milk bread finely chopped with the boned sardines, chopped chives, grated *primosale* cheese, a pinch of marjoram, lemon and orange juice, season with salt and knead together. Use this stuffing to fill the pockets in the swordfish medallions.

Place the parcels in a pan, add salt and extra virgin olive oil, pour in the white wine and roast in the oven at 150°C (300°F) for about 14 minutes.

For the garnish:
Heat the extra virgin olive oil in a pan, sauté the mushrooms and carrots, adding the peeled tomatoes. Finally, remove them from the heat and add the chives.

For the ricotta mousse:
Pass the ricotta through a sieve, add the whipped cream and season with salt. Place in the fridge and use before serving.

Composition:
Place the parcels on the plate with the side dishes, place the salad on the plate to be seasoned with extra virgin olive oil and the finely filleted orange. Lastly, mix the ricotta and whipped cream and use a pastry bag to add the mousse.

Dishes & Salads

Duck breast with Sicilian citrus and rabbit terrine

Ingredients for the duck breast:
2 duck breasts with the skin
350 g (12 oz) salt
150 g (5.3 oz) sugar
3.3 g ($^3/_5$ tsp) grated zest of mandarin,
orange and Lemon

Ingredients for the rabbit terrine:
300 g (11 oz) rabbit flesh
60 g (2.1 oz) chicken flesh
2 g ($^2/_5$ tsp) chives
40 g (1.4 oz) cream
3 g ($^2/_3$ tsp) grated mandarin peel
40 g (1.4 oz) rabbit giblets
65 g (2.3 oz) boiled peas
40 g (1.4 oz) red pumpkin
15 g ($^2/_4$ oz) sultanas
3 g ($^2/_3$ tsp) powdered gelatin
Salt to taste
¼ clove garlic

Ingredients for the citrus marmalade:
75 g (2.6 oz) mandarins
85 g (3 oz) oranges
90 g (3.2 oz) lemons
1.7 g ($^1/_3$ tsp) pectin
155 (5.5 oz) g sugar

Ingredients for the sweet and sour onions:
125 g (4.4 oz) red onions
63 (2.2 oz) g sugar
35 g (1.2 oz) vinegar
3 g ($^2/_3$ tsp) orange zest
2 g ($^2/_5$ tsp) calamint leaves
1 clove garlic

Dishes & Salads

For a festive evening, to amaze your friends, here is a moderately elaborate dish, which is certain to be a success. A fusion of flavors to set your palate dancing.

–

For the duck breast:
Mix the salt with the sugar and the grated zest of citrus fruits. Immerse the duck breasts in the salting mixture, place in a container with a drip tray, cover and refrigerate for 12 hours. When the "salting" is done, clean the duck breasts and remove them from the salt mixture. Use a small knife to score the skin and place the breasts resting on the side with the skin in a non-stick pan and heat on the hob, cover and continue to cook. When cooked, allow to cool. Before serving, cut the breast into slices.

For the rabbit terrine:
Cut 200 g (7 oz) of rabbit flesh and the pumpkin into cubes of about 1x1cm (0.4x0.4 in), salt lightly and mix with mandarin, lemon, rosemary and a quarter of a minced garlic clove. Pass the rest of the rabbit flesh, chicken, cream and some ice cubes through the cutter. Pass the mixture through a sieve, add the chopped spring onion, sultanas, cooked but crispy peas, red pumpkin, powdered gelatin, cubes of rabbit flesh and salt as required.
Put the mixture in a terrine mold, seal well and bake at 140°C (285°F) until done. Cool, cut and serve.

For the citrus marmalade:
Wash and blanch the citrus fruit for 1 minute in salted water (20 g per liter). Drain the fruit, chop and combine with sugar and pectin. Cook at 106°C (222°F). Allow to cool and serve.

Dishes & Salads

For the sweet and sour onions:
Clean and julienne the onions. Soak the onions in water and vinegar for 30 minutes and then drain. Separately add the vinegar with the sugar and cook. As soon as it simmers add a clove of garlic and the julienned onion till it is done, taking care the onion is al dente. Remove the onion from the liquid and continue to cook the sweet and sour dressing reducing it by about 25 percent. When cooked, dip the julienned onions into the sweet and sour dressing and allow to cool.

Composition:
Serve the sliced duck with the citrus marmalade. Place the salad separately on the plate and position the terrine accompanying it with the sweet and sour onions. Garnish the dish with walnut kernels and segments of orange and lemon.

Duck breast with Sicilian citrus and rabbit terrine

Desserts & Cocktails

Cannoli with orange cream **p. 118**
Frutta Martorana **p. 120**
Orange peel with chocolate **p. 121**
Danish pastry with orange **p. 124**
Meringue and cream slice with Sicilian lemons **p. 126**
Candied fruit - Mandarin or orange **p. 128**
Lemon granita **p. 132**
Salted orange ice cream **p. 133**
Cocktail with citrus fruits **p. 134**
Centrifuged orange and lotus **p. 135**
Centifuged orange and watermelon **p. 138**
Prickly pear cocktail **p. 139**

Desserts & Cocktails

Cannoli with orange cream

This is the supreme Sicilian pastry. Our version is mignon cannoli with orange cream and orange peel.

—

Ingredients for the Cannoli:
200 g (7 oz) flour
22 g (0.78 oz) eggs
20 g (0.7 oz) lard
50 g (1.8 oz) white wine vinegar
2 g ($^2/_5$ tsp) cocoa
20 g (0.7 oz) sugar
14 g (0.5 oz) cinnamon powder

Ingredients for the cream:
40 g (1.4 oz) starch
80 g (2.8 oz) sugar
Vanilla to taste
140 g (5 oz) yolk
400 g (14 oz) milk
105 g (3.7 oz) glucose

—

Method for the Cannoli:
Mix all the ingredients in a mixer at low speed. Let the dough rest for one night. Spread it very thin and cut out into ovals. Wrap around wooden or aluminum sticks and fry in oil at 170°C (338°F).

Method for the cream:
Weigh the starch, sugar, vanilla and egg yolks and mix. In a pan, bring the milk and glucose to the boil. Add the weighed ingredients a little at a time and lower the heat, stirring all the time and taking care the mixture does not stick to the pan. At the first sign of boiling, remove from the hob and spread on a small baking sheet. Cover with kitchen film and leave to cool in the fridge.

Info: To flavor it with orange, use the Danish orange recipe (for the filling) and lighten it with 400 g (14 oz) of cream whipped with 30 g (1.1 oz) of sugar.

Desserts & Cocktails

Frutta Martorana

Ingredients:
650 g (23 oz) almond powder
300 g (11 oz) sugar
400 g (14 oz) soft fondant
100 g (3.5 oz) honey
200 g (7 oz) glucose
150 g (5.3 oz) of water
450 g (16 oz) icing sugar

–

Put the almond powder in the planetary mixer with the sugar.

In a saucepan raise the fondant, honey, glucose and water to 115°C (240°F) and pour it into a planetary mixer.

Add the icing sugar and let it run at low speed until the mixture cools.

Leave it to rest and form it into balls to be shaped in plaster molds.

Add coloring.

Desserts & Cocktails
Orange peel with chocolate

Ingredients:
200 g (7 oz) organic orange peel
200 g (7 oz) water
Dark chocolate

—

Wash the oranges and cut out the area around the stem and navel. Then remove the peel, being careful not to damage it, and slicing it into segments regular in shape and height.

Put the peel in a pan with plenty of cold water, bring to the boil and change the water. Repeat this method three times, so as to eliminate the bitter taste of the albedo (pith).

Afterwards, cut the rind into matchsticks and leave it to drain on a grille for a couple of hours. Soften the dark chocolate at 31°C (88°F).

Dip the peel in the chocolate and allow it to crystallize at room temperature.

Desserts & Cocktails
Danish pastry with orange

Ingredients for the pastry:
280 g (10 oz) flour
50 g (1.8 oz) brewer's yeast
120 g (4.2 oz) eggs
26 g (0.9 oz) honey
4 g (1tsp) salt
30 g (1.1 oz) sugar
40 g (1.4 oz) butter to browse

Ingredients for the orange filling:
100 g (3.5 oz) orange
75 g (2.6 oz) sugar

Desserts & Cocktails

A sweet breakfast with a Sicilian flavor: the filling of diced orange will give you a boost in the morning.

–

Method for the pastry:
Dissolve the yeast in the eggs and knead together all the ingredients except the butter. Once you have a smooth, elastic dough, form it into a ball and leave it in the fridge until it doubles in volume.

Meanwhile spread the butter with a rolling pin to form a flat base a few millimeters thick and place it in the fridge to firm. Roll out the dough three times the width of the butter. Place the butter in the center and fold the flaps of dough over the butter. Repeat this step three times at 45 min intervals. Then roll out the dough and form to your liking.

Method for the orange filling:
Take an orange and make holes in the peel with a fork. Boil the orange for 5 minutes. When it has cooled, pass it through the meat grinder. Then put it in a pan, and for every 100 g (3.5 oz) of orange, add 75 g (2.6 oz) of sugar and bring to the boil. Once it cools, use it to flavor the pastry.

Desserts & Cocktails

Meringue and cream slice with Sicilian lemons

Ingredients for the slice:
90 g (3.2 oz) butter
30 g (1.1 oz) veil sugar
12 g (0.4 oz) egg white
90 g (3.2 oz) flour
30 g (1.1 oz) potato starch

Ingredients for the the lemon cream:
70 g (2.5 oz) egg yolks
160 g (5.6 oz) sugar
70 g (2.5 oz) lemon juice
8 g (1²/4) water
5 g (1 tsp) animal gelatin
210 g (7.4 oz) soft butter

Ingredients for the meringue:
30 g (1.1 oz) water
90 g (3.2 oz) sugar
60 g (2.1 oz) egg white

Desserts & Cocktails

**Tasty slices with meringue and lemon cream. At every bite you will relish the flavor and intense aroma of the typical Sicilian fruit.
A perfect pastry for a traditional afternoon tea.**

—

Method for the slice:
First mix the butter and sugar, then add the egg white, trickling it in slowly, and finally quickly add the flour and starch previously sifted together. Allow it to rest and form into baskets. Bake at 190°C (374°F) for eight minutes.

Method for the the lemon cream:
Mix the egg yolks, sugar, juice and water. Bring to the boil and add the gelatin.
Finally add the butter and mix with a whisk until it is blended smoothly.
Place in the fridge and allow it to rest. Whip before use.
The cream will be used to fill the pastry baskets once they are baked.

Method for the meringue:
Bring the water and sugar to 121°C (250°F), then pour it into a planetary mixer, gently trickling in the egg whites and mix until it cools. Then use it to fill a sac à poche and decorate it as in the illustrations. Use a lighter to create a singed effect.

Desserts & Cocktails

Candied fruit - Mandarin or orange

Candied citrus fruits come to us from Arab culture. This is a simple way to preserve fruit. Use candied fruit to decorate your cakes or stuff your muffins, for example.

—

Ingredients:
Peel of an orange
Salt to taste
1l (1 US quart) water
700 g (25 oz) sugar
Fruit to taste (mandarin or orange)

—

Use a toothpick to make six holes in the peel of an orange, blanch in water and salt, drain and cool.

Prepare a syrup with 1 liter of water and 600 g (21 oz) of sugar, bring to the boil and pour hot over the fruit placed in a container so it is immersed in the syrup. Let it stand for 24 hours.

Remove the syrup without moving the fruit. Add 100 g (3.5 oz) of sugar to the syrup and pour it over the fruit, then let it stand for 24 hours. Repeat this step for 10 days. On the eleventh day remove the syrup, add 10 percent of glucose and bring to the boil. Place the drained fruit in some jars and pour in the hot syrup. Cover the jars and turn upside down.

Pasteurize in boiling water for 20–40 minutes depending on the size of the fruit and the jar. Cool in running water.

Desserts & Cocktails

Lemon granita

When the heat is suffocating, only a handmade lemon granita can give you respite, a simple and safe ally.

Ingredients for the granita:
150 g (5.3 oz) sugar
150 g (5.3 oz) lemon
500 g (18 oz) water

–

Mix everything together and leave in the freezer.

Stir it from time to time as it sets.

Desserts & Cocktails
Salted orange ice cream

An original recipe for a different kind of ice-cream, a breath of summer freshness. To be served with a seafood salad or prawns.

Ingredients for the ice cream:
207 g (7.3 oz) of water
158 g (5.6 oz) brown sugar
27 g (0.95 oz) glucose
325 g (11 oz) orange juice (pulp)
1 g (¼ tsp) salt

–

Mix all the ingredients carefully, then put them in the ice-cream maker or the food processor or, if you don't have this equipment, put them in the freezer and stir frequently so that it does not form a block of ice but a creamy mass.
If you use this last method, the ice cream will be rather lumpy.

Desserts & Cocktails
Cocktail with citrus fruits
An amber-colored drink, glamorous, revitalizing and charged with energy.

Ingredients for the cocktail:
5 cl (1 ¾ oz) London Dry Gin
3 cl (1 oz) citrus juice
2 cl (²/₃ oz) black-bee honey
Soda top
2 slices of orange

—

Juice the citrus fruits (lemon and mandarin orange) in a juicer, reserving a couple of whole segments of each.

In a glass with ice add the juice of the filtered citrus fruit, two slices of orange and lemon, then pour 5 cl (1 ¾ oz) London Dry Gin, 2 cl (²/₃ oz) black-bee honey, and complete the glass with Soda top.

Desserts & Cocktails

Centrifuged orange and lotus

Orange and lotus, and even mandarin: create your own cocktail and have fun creating and looking for new and colorful containers where you can pour and shake your drink.

Ingredients for the cocktail:
2 lotus flowers
2 oranges
A few mint leaves
Crushed ice
Brown sugar to taste
1 lime

–

Juice the lotuses and oranges (peeling them and removing the pith).

Shake with crushed ice.

Crush two mint leaves with brown sugar in a glass, add a few drops of lime and then pour in the juice.

Desserts & Cocktails

Centifuged orange and watermelon

Fresh and aromatic aperitif, for a riot of delicate summery tastes.

Ingredients for the cocktail:
½ cucumber
200 g (7 oz) watermelon
1 orange
Crushed ice
A sprig of rosemary

—

Juice in a centrifuge and mix.

Serve with crushed ice and a sprig of rosemary.

Desserts & Cocktails
Prickly pear cocktail
A drink with an intense color and rich flavor.

Ingredients for the cocktail:
5 cl (1¾ oz) Cubano Añejo rum
2 cl (⅔ oz) lemon juice
2 cl (⅔ oz) puree of prickly pear
2 bar spoons of Violetta

–

Gently mix 5 cl (1¾ oz) Cubano Añejo rum, 2 cl (⅔ oz) lemon juice, 2 cl (⅔ oz) puree of prickly pear.

Then pour everything in a glass chilled with ice and add 2 tablespoons of Violetta.

2018 © SIME BOOKS
All rights reserved

Texts and historical research
Vinci Bellomo
Translation
Richard Sadleir
Design
Jenny Biffis
Illustration
Salvo Scherma, Monica Parussolo
Prepress
Fabio Mascanzoni

All images were taken by Antonino Bartuccio and Alessandro Saffo except for:
Ferruccio Carassale p. 57, Matteo Carassale p. 6, 53, Gabriele Croppi p. 62, Guido Cozzi p. 84, Paolo Giocoso p. 131, Laurent Grandadam p. 27, Johanna Huber p. 7, 56, Thelma&Louise p. 49, Aldo Pavan p. 130, Giovanni Simeone p. 13, 16, 30

Photos available on www.simephoto.com

Special thanks for the recipes:
Pasticceria Delizia di Bolognetta, Tenuta Scozzari Ricevimenti Bolognetta, Villeroy Resort Ricevimenti, Bolognetta, Mauro Lo Faso, Giuseppe Giuliano, Francesco Lo Faso, Tommaso Meschisi, Dario Arena, Gianluca Di Giorgio

Bibliography:
Storia degli Agrumi – *Pierre Laszlo* – Donzelli editore, 2006, Conca d'oro – *Giuseppe Barbera* – Sellerio editore, 2012, La terra che nutre – *Autori Vari* - Giunti, 2013, La favolosa storia degli Agrumi – *Francesco Calabrese* - L'Epos, 2004, Arancia – *Carmelo Chiaramonte* – Elvira Assenza – Edizioni Estemporanee, 2012, Dove fiorisce il limone – *Antonino Buttitta* – Sellerio, 1984, Bagheria operosa – *Emanuele Nicosia* – Comune di Bagheria, 2010

ISBN 978-88-99180-38-6
Sime srl - www.simebooks.com